table of contents

intro by susan b. anderson..................7

dolls and outfits.......................8-14

patterns

    doll 16

    cozy shawl 25

    comfy cardi 26

    pretty dress 28

    fancy skirt 30

standard abbreviations...................32

bios 33

Mary, Millie, and Morgan are knitted seamlessly from the top down. When you knit the last stitch, you're as good as done. Add a simple little face by way of a few embroidery stitches, two beautiful braids, and you've created a doll that will be filled with memories for your beloved little ones.

My love of dolls and children and dreams and the pure playfulness of childhood makes this doll set extra dear to me. Thinking about mamas, papas, and grandmas making little sets of wool dolls to keep, cherish, and pass on for generations means more than words can say... Enjoy!

Mary   Morgan   Millie

in our comfy cardis

& fancy skirts,

dressed up...

in pretty dresses,

wrapped up in cozy shawls,

and always in our birthday suits.

the patterns

Mary, Millie, and Morgan
Susan B. Anderson

Finished measurements
9" [23 cm] tall when standing, 6" [15 cm] body circumference, approx 3½" [9 cm] arm length, and 4½" [11.5 cm] leg length

Yarn
Chickadee by Quince & Co
(100% American wool; 181yd [166m]/50g
- 1 skein each in the following colorways:

Doll #1 (Millie):
Egret 101, Bird's Egg 106, Frank's Plum 114, Storm 104, Winesap 133, Glacier 105, and Carrie's Yellow 125

Doll #2 (Mary):
Petal 111, Carrie's Yellow 125, Kumlien's Gull 152, Gingerbread 120, Crow 102, and Lupine 116

Doll #3 (Morgan):
Twig 119, Iceland 153, Peacock 109, Crow 102, and Winesap 133

Note: Leftover yarn can be used for outfits.

Needles
- One set of 4 double-pointed needles (dpns) in size US 3 [3.25 mm]

Or size to obtain gauge

Notions
- Removable stitch markers
- Waste yarn
- Natural wool or fiberfill for stuffing
- Tapestry needle
- Black and red embroidery floss (separated into 1 or 2 strands) or Perle Cotton

Gauge
6½ sts = 1" [2.5 cm] inch in stockinette stitch.

Special abbreviations
k1-f/b (knit 1, front and back): Knit into the front loop, then the back loop of next st (1 st increased).
ssk (slip, slip, knit): Slip 2 sts one at a time knitwise to the RH needle; return sts to LH needle in turned position and knit them together through the back loops (1 st decreased, leans to the left).
k2tog: Knit 2 sts together (1 st decreased, leans to the right).
p2tog: Purl 2 sts together (1 st decreased).
sl 1: Slip next st purlwise with yarn to wrong side of work.

Stockinette Stitch (St st)
Knit every round.

Backward loop cast on
*Wrap yarn around left thumb from front to back and secure in palm with other fingers. Insert needle upwards through strand on thumb. Slip loop from thumb onto RH needle, pulling yarn to tighten. Rep from * for desired number of sts.

Helpful links
For instructions on the **long-tail cast on**, we like: www.knitty.com/ISSUEsummer05/FEATsum05TT.html
For instructions on embroidering **French knots**, see: www.sublimestitching.com/pages/how-to-french-knot
For **duplicate stitch**, we like: www.knitty.com/ISSUEfall04/FEATfall04TT.html

Note
The doll is worked seamlessly from the top down, starting at the top of the head. The head is shaped first by increases, then decreases to form the neck. The shoulders and yoke are worked similarly to a top-down sweater by increasing to the underarm. The arms are held on waste yarn while the body and legs are worked down to the shoes. The arm stitches are then picked up and worked down to the hands.

Doll

Head

Starting at the top of the head with the selected skin color, smaller dpn, and using the long-tail cast on, CO 9 sts, placing 3 stitches on each of 3 dpns. Join to work in the round, being careful not to twist stitches. Place a stitch marker on the first stitch.

Rnd 1: Knit.
Rnd 2 *inc rnd*: *K1-f/b; rep from * to end of rnd—6 sts per needle, 18 sts total.
Rnds 3 and 4: Knit.
Rnd 5 *inc rnd*: *K1-f/b; rep from * to end of rnd—12 sts per needle, 36 sts total.
Place a stitch marker on stitch from Rnd 5 and leave it there. Knit every round until the head measures 1¼" [3 cm] below the stitch marker on Rnd 5.

Decrease for neck

Rnd 1 *dec rnd*: *K4, k2tog; rep from *—10 sts per needle, 30 sts total.
Rnd 2 *dec rnd*: *K3, k2tog; rep from *—8 sts per needle, 24 sts total.
Rnd 3: Knit.
Rnd 4 *dec rnd*: *K2, k2tog; rep from *—6 sts per needle, 18 sts total.
Rnd 5: Knit.
Rnd 6 *dec rnd*: *K1, k2tog; rep from *—4 sts per needle, 12 sts total.
Rnd 7: Knit.

At this point, thread the cast-on tail onto a tapestry needle and make small gathering stitches along the cast-on edge to close the hole at the top of the head. Pull the end to the inside and trim. Stuff the head and neck with natural wool roving or fiberfill. Continue stuffing as needed as the doll progresses.

Torso

Switch to the selected shirt color.
Rnd 1 *inc rnd*: *K1-f/b, k2, k1-f/b; rep from *—6 sts per needle, 18 sts total.
Rnd 2: Knit.
Rnd 3 *inc rnd*: *K2, k1-f/b; rep from *—8 sts per needle, 24 sts total.
Rnd 4: Knit.
Rnd 5 *inc rnd*: *K1, k1-f/b; rep from *—12 sts per needle, 36 sts total.
Rnds 6-8: Knit.
Rnd 9 *inc rnd*: *K2, k1-f/b; rep from *—16 sts per needle, 48 sts total.
Rnd 10: Knit.
Rnd 11 *inc rnd*: *K3, k1-f/b; rep from *—20 sts per needle, 60 sts total.

Separate body and arms
Next rnd:
Needle 1 (N1): K10, place the next 10 sts on waste yarn, then with the backward loop cast on, CO 2 sts—12 sts;
Needle 2 (N2): Knit 20 sts;
Needle 3 (N3): Place the first 10 sts on waste yarn, then with the backward loop cast on, CO 2 sts, k10—12 sts (44 sts total).
Note: Needle 2 is the front of the body.
Knit every round until the body measures ¾" [2 cm] below the armhole.

Begin waist shaping
Next rnd dec rnd:
(N1) Knit to the last 2 stitches, ssk—11 sts;
(N2) K2tog, knit to the last 2 stitches, ssk—18 sts;
(N3) K2tog, knit to the end of the round—11 sts (40 sts total).
Knit 2 rounds even.
Switch to the first color for the striped tights.
Knit 6 rounds even.
Next rnd dec rnd: *K3, k2tog; rep from *—32 sts.
Stuff the body and waist until firm. Do not overstuff.

Divide for legs
Place the first 16 stitches on waste yarn for the right leg.
Note: Hold the doll with the back facing you, so she's looking in the same direction you are. The right and left for the doll are referred to with the back of the doll facing you.

Left leg
Place the next 16 stitches for the left leg on 3 dpns as follows: (N1 and N2) 4 sts each; (N3) 8 sts.
Join to work in the round. Place a stitch marker on the first stitch (at the center).
Knit one round.

Begin striped tights
Switch to second color for striped tights.
Rnds 1-5: Knit.
Switch colors.
Rnds 6-10: Knit.
Switch colors.
Repeat Rnds 1-10 until there are 3 stripes of each color or 6 stripes total.
Stuff the leg.

Left shoe
Switch to the selected shoe color.

Heel flap
Working back and forth on the 8 sts on N3 only, turn to purl.
Row 1: (WS) Sl 1, purl.
Row 2: Sl 1, knit.
Rows 3-6: Rep Rows 1 and 2.
Next row *dec row:* (WS) Sl 1, p4, p2tog, p1, turn.

Next row *dec row:* Sl 1, k3, k2tog, k1.
This is now N1.
6 sts remain.

Gusset
With a free dpn, pick up and knit 4 sts on the left side of the heel flap.
Combine the stitches on the next two dpns onto one dpn. This is now N2.
Knit across the 8 sts on N2.
With an empty dpn, pick up and knit 4 sts on the right side of the heel flap. This is now N3.
Knit 3 sts from N1 onto N3.
Place the remaining 3 sts onto N1.
Place a stitch marker on the first stitch on N1.
(N1 and N3) 7 sts each; (N2) 8 sts — 22 sts total.
Begin working in the round.

Foot
First rnd: Knit.
Next rnd *dec rnd:* (N1) Knit to the last 2 sts, k2tog; (N2) Knit; (N3) Ssk, knit to the end — 20 sts.
Repeat last 2 rnds one more time — (N1 and N3) 5 sts; (N2) 8 sts — 18 sts total.
Knit every round until the foot measures 1½" [4 cm] from the back of the heel.
Stuff the foot.

Toe
Rearrange the stitches so 6 sts are on each needle.
First rnd *dec rnd:* *K1, k2tog; rep from * — 12 sts.
Next rnd: Knit.
Next rnd *dec rnd:* *K2tog; rep from * — 6 sts.
Finish any remaining stuffing.
Cut the yarn and thread the tail on a tapestry needle. Pull the tail through the remaining stitches and pull up tight to close the hole. Pull tail to the inside and trim.

Right leg
Place held stitches on three dpns as follows:
(N1) 8 sts; (N2 and N3) 4 sts each.
Reattach the same color yarn to begin working on N1, leaving a 6" [15 cm] tail to use later to close the gap between the legs. Place a stitch marker on the first stitch of N1.
Knit one round.
Begin the striped tights and work the same as the left leg to the shoe.

Right shoe
Switch to the selected shoe color.
Knit across N1, turn.

Heel flap
Work back and forth on the 8 sts on N1 only.
Row 1: (WS) Sl 1, purl.
Row 2: Sl 1, knit.
Rows 3-6: Rep Rows 1 and 2.
Next row *dec row:* (WS) Sl 1, p4, p2tog, p1, turn.
Next row *dec row:* Sl 1, k3, k2tog, k1.
6 sts remain.

Gusset
With a free dpn, pick up and knit 4 sts on the left side of the heel flap.
Combine the stitches on N2 and N3 onto one dpn. This is now N2.
Knit across the 8 sts on N2.
With a free dpn, pick up and knit 4 sts on the right side of the heel flap. This is now N3.
Knit 3 sts from N1 onto N3.
Place the remaining 3 sts onto N1.
Place a stitch marker on the first stitch on N1.
Begin working in the round.
(N1 and N3) 7 sts each; (N2) 8 sts—22 sts total.
Begin working in the round.

Foot
First rnd: Knit.
Next rnd *dec rnd:* (N1) Knit to the last 2 sts, k2tog; (N2) Knit; (N3) Ssk, knit to the end—20 sts.
Repeat last 2 rnds one more time—(N1 and N3) 5 sts; (N2) 8 sts—18 sts total.
Knit every round until the foot measures 1½" [4 cm] from the back of the heel.
Stuff the foot.

Toe
Rearrange the stitches so 6 sts are on each needle.
First rnd *dec rnd:* *K1, k2tog; rep from *—12 sts.
Next rnd: Knit.
Next rnd *dec rnd:* *K2tog; rep from *—6 sts.
Finish any remaining stuffing.
Cut the yarn and thread the tail on a tapestry needle. Pull the tail through the remaining stitches and pull up tight to close the hole. Pull tail to the inside and trim.

Arm
Place all held stitches for one arm on dpns as follows: (N1 and N2) 4 sts each; (N3) 2 sts.
Reattach skin color and begin to knit on N1.
First rnd: Knit to the end of N3, then with same needle, pick up and knit 4 more stitches—14 sts.
Next rnd *dec rnd:* Knit to N3, then on N3, k2, (k2tog) two times—4 sts per needle, 12 sts total.
Knit every round until the arm measures 2½" [5 cm] from underarm.
Stuff the arm.

Hand
Rnd 1 *dec rnd:* *K2, k2tog; rep from *—3 sts per needle, 9 sts total.
Rnd 2 *dec rnd:* *K1, k2tog; rep from *—2 sts per needle, 6 sts total.
Rnd 3 *inc rnd:* *K1-f/b; rep from *—4 sts per needle, 12 sts total.
Rnds 4-8: Knit.
Rnd 9 *dec rnd:* *K2, k2tog; rep from *—3 sts per needle, 9 sts total.
Rep for other arm.
Finish stuffing the arms and hands. Cut the yarn and thread tail on tapestry needle. Pull tail through the remaining stitches and tighten to close the hole. Pull tail to the inside and trim.

Finishing
Ears
With dpn and selected skin color, pick up 3 stitches ¾" [2 cm] above the start of the shirt and to the side of the head. Pick up by inserting the needle under the right leg of 3 consecutive stitches in the same column.
With 2nd dpn, knit 1 row.
Next row: Bind off.
Cut the yarn and thread tail on tapestry needle. Pull tail to the inside and trim. Repeat with the first tail.

Face detail
Eyes: Thread a 12" [30.5 cm] length of black embroidery floss or Perle Cotton on a tapestry needle.
Make 2 French knots, spacing them ¾" [2 cm] apart and slightly above mid-line of face.
Nose: Thread a 12" [30.5 cm] strand of skin color yarn on tapestry needle. Take two tiny straight stitches right next to each other for the nose.
Mouth: With red embroidery floss or Perle Cotton, make 3 tiny straight stitches to form a slight smile.
Eyebrows: With a strand of the selected hair color yarn, make a tiny straight stitch above each eye.

Hair
Cut 15" [38 cm] strands of the selected hair color as you apply the hair (this way you can add more as you go and won't cut too many lengths).
Place 2 strands held together on a tapestry needle. Find the center of the forehead about 5 rows above the eyebrows. Pull the two strands held together under a stitch, halfway through, leaving the ends on either side of the center part. Continue pulling the strands under consecutive stitches from the front of the hairline down to the hairline at the back of the neck.

Wrap a strand of the hair color yarn several times around the hair at the base of the head on each side to form two ponytails and secure by going under a few stitches on the head. Then braid each side and tie ends with matching hair color yarn.

With another strand of yarn in the hair color, and starting at the front of the part, make little straight stitches to cover the exposed knit stitch all along the part of the hair. Pull the end to the inside and trim.

Shoe detail (to create maryjanes)
With a strand of skin-color yarn, work duplicate stitch over three rows of three stitches and one stitch in the center of the three stitches on the fourth row close to the toe.

Cozy Shawl

Finished measurements
10" [25.5 cm] wingspan and 3½" [9 cm] long at center spine

Yarn
Chickadee by Quince & Co
(100% American wool; 181yd [166m]/50g)
Shown in Iceland 153; Lupine 116; and Frank's Plum 114

Needles
- Two double-pointed needles (dpns) in size US 5 [3.75 mm]

Or size to obtain gauge

Notions
- Stitch markers (m)
- Stitch holders or waste yarn
- Tapestry needle

Gauge
6 sts = 1" [2.5 cm] in stockinette stitch, after blocking.

Special abbreviations

yo (yarn over): Bring yarn between needles to the front, then over RH needle ready to knit the next st (1 st increased).
k2tog: Knit 2 sts together (1 st decreased, leans to the right).

Stockinette stitch (St st)
Knit on the RS, purl on the WS.

I-cord
With RS facing, knit sts on dpn. Do not turn work. Slide sts to right end of dpn, ready to knit the next row.

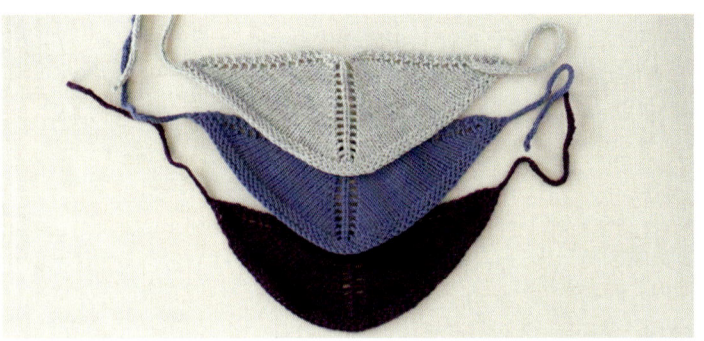

Shawl
Begin at center back neck
With selected shawl color and using the long-tail cast on, CO 9 sts.

Row 1: (RS) K2, place marker (pm), k2, pm, k1, pm, k2, pm, k2.

Row 2: K2, purl to last marker (m), k2.

Row 3 *inc row*: K2, slip marker (sl m), yo, knit to m, yo, sl m, k1, sl m, yo, knit to m, yo, sl m, k2 (4 sts inc'd)—13 sts.

Repeat Rows 2 and 3 until there are 61 sts total, ending after Row 2.

Knit 4 rows.

Next row: Bind off as follows:
K2, place these 2 sts on waste yarn or a stitch holder, bind off loosely to the last 2 sts.

Ties
Place these last 2 sts on a dpn. Using 2 dpns, work in i-cord for 6" [15 cm].

Next row: K2tog—1 st rem.

Cut yarn and pull tail through the remaining stitch.
Weave in the end.
Place the first two held sts on a dpn. Work the second tie same as the first.

Finishing
Weave in ends and trim. Steam- or wet-block to measurements.

Comfy Cardi
Finished measurements
7" [18 cm] body width

Yarn
Chickadee by Quince & Co
(100% American wool; 181yd [166m]/50g)
Shown in Peacock 109; Winesap 133; and Kumlien's Gull 152

Needles
- One set of double-pointed needles (dpns) in size US 3 [3.25 mm]*

Or size to obtain gauge

*The sample was knit entirely on 6" dpns, working back and forth on 2 dpns and then working the sleeves in the round on 3 dpns.

Notions
- Stitch markers
- Waste yarn
- Two 3/8" buttons
- Sewing needle and thread
- Tapestry needle

Gauge
6½ sts = 1" [2.5 cm] in garter stitch, after blocking.

Special abbreviations
k1-f/b (knit 1, front and back): Knit into the front loop, then the back loop of next st (1 st increased).
yo (yarn over): Bring yarn between needles to the front, then over RH needle ready to knit the next st (1 st increased).
k2tog: Knit 2 sts together (1 st decreased, leans to the right).
p2tog: Purl 2 sts together (1 st decreased).

Garter stitch
Knit every row.

Backward loop cast on
*Wrap yarn around left thumb from front to back and secure in palm with other fingers. Insert needle upwards through strand on thumb. Slip loop from thumb onto RH needle, pulling yarn to tighten. Rep from * for desired number of sts.

Cardigan
Begin at neck
With selected cardigan color and using the long-tail cast on, CO 24 stitches as follows: CO 4, place marker (pm), CO 2, pm, CO 12, pm, CO 2, pm, CO 4.
Row 1 *inc row*: (RS) *Knit to 1 st before the marker (m), k1-f/b, sl m, k1-f/b; repeat from * 3 more times, knit to end (8 sts inc'd)—32 sts.
Row 2: Knit.
Row 3 *buttonhole row*: *Knit to 1 st before the marker, k1-f/b, sl m, k1-f/b; repeat from * 3 more times, knit to the last 3 sts, k2tog, yo, k1—40 sts.
Row 4: Knit.
Rows 5-10: Repeat Rows 1 and 2—64 sts.
Row 11 *buttonhole row and separate sleeves and body*: Knit to m, remove m, slip next 12 sts for sleeve onto waste yarn, remove m, CO 3 sts using the backward loop cast on, knit to next m, remove m, slip the next 12 sts for sleeve onto waste yarn, remove m, CO 3 sts using the backward loop cast on, knit to the last 3 sts, k2tog, yo, k1—46 body sts.

Next row: Knit.
Cont in garter stitch until the cardigan measures 1½" [4 cm] below the underarm.
Next row: Bind off.

Sleeves
Place the 12 held stitches onto 3 dpns with 4 sts on each needle. Join yarn and knit 12 sts, then with N3, pick up and knit 4 more stitches from the underarm—16 sts:
(N1 and N2) 4 sts; (N3) 8 sts.
Next rnd *dec rnd*: (N1 and N2) Purl; (N3) P4, (p2tog) twice (2 sts dec'd)—14 sts rem.
Continue with the sleeve as follows:

Next rnd: Knit.
Next rnd: Purl.
Repeat the last 2 rnds until sleeve measures 2½" [5 cm] from the underarm. **Next rnd**: Bind off loosely.

Finishing
Weave in ends and trim. Steam- or wet-block to measurements. Sew on two tiny buttons across from the buttonholes.

Pretty Dress

Finished measurements
7" [18 cm] chest circumference and 4" [10 cm] long

Yarn
Chickadee by Quince & Co
(100% American wool; 181yd [166m]/50g)
One-color version shown in Crow 102 and Frank's Plum 114
Striped version shown in Crow 102; Iceland 153; and Winesap 133

Needles
- One set of 5 double-pointed needles (dpns) in size US 5 [3.75 mm]

Or size to obtain gauge

Notions
- Removable stitch marker
- Waste yarn
- Tapestry needle

Gauge
6 sts = 1" [2.5 cm] in stockinette stitch, after blocking.

Special abbreviation
k1-f/b (knit 1, front and back): Knit into the front loop, then the back loop of next st (1 st increased).

Stockinette stitch (St st)
Knit every round.

Dress
Begin at neck
With the selected dress color and using the long-tail cast on, CO 24 sts, placing 8 sts on each of 3 dpns. Join to work in the round being careful not to twist the stitches. Place a stitch marker on the first stitch.

Rnd 1: Knit.
Rnd 2: Purl.
Rnd 3 *inc rnd*: *K1, k1-f/b; rep from * to end of rnd—12 sts per needle, 36 sts total.
Rnds 4-6: Knit.
Rnd 7 *inc rnd*: *K2, k1-f/b; rep from *—16 sts per needle, 48 sts total.
Rnd 8: Knit.
Rnd 9 *inc rnd*: *K3, k1-f/b; rep from *—20 sts per needle, 60 sts total.

Separate body and sleeves
Rnd 1: (N1) K10, place the next 10 sts on waste yarn, then with the backward loop cast on, CO 3—13 sts; (N2) Knit 20 sts; (N3) Place first 10 sts on waste yarn, then with the backward loop cast on, CO 3, k10—13 sts (46 sts total).
Rnds 2 and 3: Knit.
Rnd 4: Purl.
Knit every round until the dress measures 2¼" [6 cm] below Rnd 4.
Note: If adding stripes, work 2 rounds in the main color after the purl round. Join contrast color and work in two-round stripes alternating colors and carrying the colors on the inside. If desired, change to a third color for the bind off.

Bottom edging
Rnd 1: Purl.
Rnd 2: Knit.
Rnd 3: Purl.
Next rnd: Bind off loosely.

Sleeves
Place 10 held sts onto 3 dpns with 4 sts on the first 2 needles and 2 sts on the third needle. Join yarn and knit the 10 sts, then pick up 3 sts from the underarm onto the third needle.

Rnds 1 and 2: Knit.
Rnd 3: Purl.
Rnd 4: Knit.
Rnd 5: Purl.
Next rnd: Bind off loosely.
Rep for other sleeve.

Finishing
Weave in ends and trim. Steam- or wet-block to measurements.

Fancy Skirt

Finished measurements
6" [15 cm] waist circumference and 3" [7.5 cm] long

Yarn
Chickadee by Quince & Co
(100% American wool; 181yd [166m]/50g)
Shown in Storm 104 (MC)/Egret 101 (CC);
Carrie's Yellow 125 (MC)/Kumlien's Gull 152 (CC);
and Winesap 133 (MC)/Peacock 109 (CC)

Needles
- One set of double-pointed needles (dpns) in size US 2 [2.75 mm]
- One set of dpns in size US 3 [3.25 mm]

Or size to obtain gauge

Notions
- Removable stitch marker
- Tapestry needle

Gauge
6½ sts = 1" [2.5 cm] in stockinette stitch on larger dpns, after blocking.

Special abbreviation
k1-f/b (knit 1, front and back): Knit into the front loop, then the back loop of next st (1 st increased).

Stockinette stitch (St st)
Knit every round.

Skirt
Begin ribbed waist
With MC, smaller dpns, and using the long-tail cast on, CO 40 sts. Place a stitch marker on the first stitch and join to work in the round, being careful not to twist stitches.
First rnd: *K2, p2; rep from * to end of rnd.
Cont in established rib until skirt measures 1" [2.5 cm] from CO edge.
Change to larger dpns.
Next rnd *inc rnd*: *K1, k1-f/b; rep from * to end—60 sts.
Continue in St st until skirt measures 2" [5 cm] from CO edge.

Begin color work pattern
Rnd 1: *K3MC, k1CC; rep from * to end.
Rnd 2: With MC, knit.
Rnd 3: *K1CC, k3MC; rep from *.
Rnd 4: *K1MC, k1CC; rep from *.
Rnd 5: *K1CC, k1MC; rep from *.
Rnd 6: *K1MC, k1CC; rep from *.
Rnds 7 and 8: With CC, knit.
Rnd 9: *With CC, k1, p1; rep from *.
Rnd 10: *With CC, p1, k1; rep from *.
Next rnd: Bind off loosely.

Finishing
Weave in ends and trim. Steam- or wet-block to measurements.

Standard abbreviations

approx	approximately	mm	millimeter(s)
beg	begin(ning); begin; begins	m(s)	marker(s)
BO	bind off	N	needle
BOR	beginning of round	p	purl
CO	cast on	patt(s)	pattern(s)
CC	contrasting color	pc(s)	piece(s)
circ	circular needle	pm	place marker
cm	centimeter(s)	rem	remain(ing)
cont	continue(s); continuing	rep	repeat; repeating
dec('d)	decrease(d)	RH	right hand
dpn(s)	double-pointed needle(s)	rnd(s)	round(s)
EOR	every other rnd	RS	right side
est	establish(ed)	sl	slip
g	gram(s)	sl m	slip marker
inc('d)	increase(d)	st(s)	stitch(es)
k	knit	St st	stockinette stitch
LH	left hand	tog	together
MC	main color	WS	wrong side
meas	measures	yd	yard(s)